# First Grade Math
# Beginners Addition & Subtraction

Speedy Publishing LLC
40 E. Main St. #1156
Newark, DE 19711
www.speedypublishing.com

# Adding 2 single-digit numbers

Solve.

1. 5 + 9 = ____
2. 2 + 9 = ____
3. 4 + 5 = ____
4. 6 + 3 = ____
5. 3 + 0 = ____
6. 3 + 9 = ____
7. 2 + 0 = ____
8. 1 + 4 = ____

**9.** 2 + 5 = ____

**10.** 9 + 1 = ____

**11.** 3 + 6 = ____

**12.** 5 + 1 = ____

**13.** 3 + 1 = ____

**14.** 2 + 1 = ____

**15.** 9 + 2 = ____

**16.** 0 + 8 = ____

**17.** 0 + 3 = ____

**18.** 9 + 7 = ____

**19.** 9 + 8 = ____

**20.** 6 + 9 = ____

**21.** 8 + 3 = ____

**22.** 1 + 3 = ____

**23.** 5 + 4 = ____

**24.** 8 + 1 = ____

**25.** 6 + 8 = ____

**26.** 8 + 7 = ____

**27.** 5 + 7 = ____

**28.** 7 + 1 = ____

**29.** 3 + 2 = ____

**30.** 4 + 6 = ____

**31.** 1 + 6 = ____

**32.** 1 + 0 = ____

**33.** 1 + 4 = ____

**34.** 7 + 5 = ____

**35.** 5 + 8 = ____

**36.** 9 + 0 = ____

**37.** 4 + 0 = ____

**38.** 4 + 7 = ____

**39.** 6 + 2 = ____

**40.** 4 + 3 = ____

**41.** 0 + 0 = ____

**42.** 4 + 4 = ____

**43.** 0 + 5 = ____

**44.** 5 + 1 = ____

**45.** 5 + 2 = ____

**46.** 8 + 0 = ____

**47.** 0 + 6 = ____

**48.** 9 + 9 = ____

**49.** 5 + 5 = ____

**50.** 8 + 8 = ____

**51.** 5 + 2 = ____

**52.** 2 + 7 = ____

**53.** 0 + 5 = ____

**54.** 1 + 2 = ____

**55.** 5 + 7 = ____

**56.** 5 + 6 = ____

# Missing Addend

**Solve.**

**1.** ___ + 5 = 13

**2.** 4 + ___ = 7

**3.** ___ + 2 = 8

**4.** ___ + 2 = 7

**5.** ______ + 10 = 20

**6.** ___ + 7 = 10

**7.** ___ + 5 = 6

**8.** ___ + 3 = 4

9. ___ + 4 = 5

10. ___ + 6 = 9

11. ___ + 5 = 10

12. ___ + 2 = 9

13. 1 + ___ = 4

14. 1 + ___ = 8

15. 3 + ___ = 7

16. 2 + ___ = 2

17. ______ + 10 = 20

18. 5 + ___ = 10

19. 1 + ___ = 7

20. 7 + ___ = 7

**21.** 3 + ___ = 3

**22.** ___ + 9 = 13

**23.** ___ + 6 = 13

**24.** 2 + ___ = 7

**25.** ___ + 9 = 18

**26.** ___ + 3 = 4

**27.** 10 + ___ = 10

**28.** 9 + ___ = 9

**29.** 6 + ___ = 7

**30.** 7 + ___ = 10

**31.** ___ + 8 = 10

**32.** 4 + ___ = 5

**33.** 0 + ___ = 5

**34.** ___ + 6 = 7

**35.** ___ + 5 = 7

**36.** 10 + ___ = 13

**37.** 5 + ___ = 6

**38.** ___ + 1 = 10

**39.** 6 + ___ = 6

**40.** 2 + ___ = 2

**41.** 9 + ___ = 16

**42.** 3 + ___ = 12

**43.** ___ + 1 = 9

**44.** ___ + 6 = 14

**45.** 10 + ___ = 18

**46.** 5 + ___ = 10

**47.** ___ + 3 = 13

**48.** ___ + 9 = 12

**49.** 8 + ___ = 15

**50.** 1 + ___ = 2

**51.** ___ + 4 = 14

**52.** ___ + 2 = 2

**53.** 6 + ___ = 14

**54.** 5 + ___ = 14

**55.** 3 + ___ = 5

**56.** 1 + ___ = 8

**57.** ___ + 2 = 7

**58.** ___ + 4 = 11

**59.** 2 + ___ = 11

**60.** ___ + 3 = 4

**61.** 2 + ___ = 12

**62.** ___ + 0 = 1

**63.** 6 + ___ = 6

**64.** 1 + ___ = 7

**65.** 10 + ___ = 11

**66.** ___ + 1 = 4

**67.** 3 + ___ = 5

**68.** 5 + ___ = 5

# Add 3 numbers within 20

Solve.

1. 5 + 5 + 1 = ____
2. 1 + 6 + 3 = ____
3. 1 + 5 + 5 = ____
4. 6 + 0 + 2 = ____
5. 6 + 3 + 9 = ____
6. 3 + 4 + 9 = ____
7. 3 + 3 + 8 = ____
8. 1 + 5 + 6 = ____

**9.** 5 + 9 + 4 = ____

**10.** 6 + 3 + 2 = ____

**11.** 3 + 4 + 8 = ____

**12.** 5 + 1 + 2 = ____

**13.** 6 + 1 + 4 = ____

**14.** 3 + 2 + 2 = ____

**15.** 3 + 0 + 8 = ____

**16.** 4 + 4 + 3 = ____

**17.** 2 + 1 + 3 = ____

**18.** 5 + 5 + 9 = ____

**19.** 5 + 1 + 1 = ____

**20.** 1 + 1 + 1 = ____

# Subtracting within 0-10

**Solve.**

**1.** 8 – 5 = ______

**2.** 3 – 3 = ______

**3.** 7 – 4 = ______

**4.** 10 – 10 = ______

**5.** 3 – 2 = ______

**6.** 9 – 3 = ______

**7.** 8 – 7 = ______

**8.** 9 – 9 = ______

**9.** 0 – 0 = ______

**10.** 9 – 2 = ______

**11.** 6 – 5 = ______

**12.** 2 – 2 = ______

**13.** 4 – 2 = ______

**14.** 6 – 6 = ______

**15.** 6 – 2 = ______

**16.** 1 – 0 = ______

**17.** 1 – 1 = ______

**18.** 9 – 0 = ______

**19.** 7 – 5 = ______

**20.** 3 – 1 = ______

21. 9 − 1 = ______

22. 4 − 1 = ______

23. 9 − 8 = ______

24. 4 − 4 = ______

25. 16 − 6 = ______

26. 6 − 0 = ______

27. 16 − 13 = ______

28. 9 − 6 = ______

29. 7 − 3 = ______

30. 5 − 2 = ______

31. 4 − 3 = ______

32. 1 − 0 = ______

**33.** 6 − 1 = ______

**34.** 8 − 7 = ______

**35.** 4 − 0 = ______

**36.** 0 − 0 = ______

**37.** 3 − 1 = ______

**38.** 6 − 4 = ______

**39.** 8 − 5 = ______

**40.** 4 − 2 = ______

**41.** 9 − 6 = ______

**42.** 3 − 0 = ______

**43.** 1 − 1 = ______

**44.** 9 − 3 = ______

**45.** 9 − 5 = ______

**46.** 2 − 0 = ______

**47.** 5 − 2 = ______

**48.** 3 − 3 = ______

**49.** 10 − 0 = ______

**50.** 6 − 6 = ______

**51.** 8 − 2 = ______

**52.** 6 − 2 = ______

**53.** 7 − 7 = ______

**54.** 4 − 4 = ______

**55.** 5 − 3 = ______

**56.** 9 − 2 = ______

**57.** 2 – 1 = ______

**58.** 10 – 10 = ______

**59.** 6 – 0 = ______

**60.** 2 – 0 = ______

**61.** 8 – 4 = ______

**62.** 7 – 7 = ______

**63.** 7 – 3 = ______

**64.** 1 – 0 = ______

**65.** 8 – 0 = ______

**66.** 8 – 8 = ______

**67.** 4 – 3 = ______

**68.** 8 – 7 = ______

# Missing Minuend or Subtrahend

**Solve.**

**1.** 8 – ______ = 8

**2.** 3 – ______ = 0

**3.** ______ – 9 = 0

**4.** 0 – ______ = 0

**5.** 5 – ______ = 4

**6.** 2 – ______ = 1

**7.** 10 – ______ = 2

**8.** ______ – 4 = 4

9. ______ − 1 = 1

10. 5 − ______ = 2

11. 3 − ______ = 3

12. ______ − 2 = 0

13. ______ − 2 = 6

14. ______ − 0 = 0

15. 8 − ______ = 3

16. ______ − 3 = 1

17. ______ − 1 = 0

18. ______ − 0 = 3

19. ______ − 1 = 5

20. 4 − ______ = 3

21. ______ − 5 = 1

22. 6 − ______ = 6

23. ______ − 0 = 1

24. 2 − ______ = 1

25. ______ − 4 = 1

26. 7 − ______ = 0

27. ______ − 3 = 6

28. 10 − ______ = 3

29. ______ − 0 = 0

30. 6 − ______ = 2

31. ______ − 4 = 0

32. 2 − ______ = 0

**33.** ______ − 5 = 4

**34.** 1 − ______ = 0

**35.** 3 − ______ = 2

**36.** ______ − 6 = 1

**37.** 8 − ______ = 5

**38.** ______ − 2 = 2

**39.** ______ − 2 = 7

**40.** 5 − ______ = 4

**41.** ______ − 3 = 0

**42.** ______ − 1 = 0

**43.** ______ − 4 = 3

**44.** 0 − ______ = 0

**45.** 5 − ______ = 2

**46.** 7 − ______ = 7

**47.** ______ − 2 = 1

**48.** 10 − ______ = 4

**49.** 9 − ______ = 0

**50.** ______ − 0 = 2

**51.** 10 − ______ = 6

**52.** 2 − ______ = 2

**53.** ______ − 5 = 0

**54.** 6 − ______ = 5

**55.** 5 − ______ = 5

**56.** 8 − ______ = 5

## Adding 2 single-digit numbers

| | | | | | | | |
|---|---|---|---|---|---|---|---|
| **1.** | 14 | **15.** | 11 | **29.** | 5 | **43.** | 5 |
| **2.** | 11 | **16.** | 8 | **30.** | 10 | **44.** | 6 |
| **3.** | 9 | **17.** | 3 | **31.** | 7 | **45.** | 7 |
| **4.** | 9 | **18.** | 16 | **32.** | 1 | **46.** | 8 |
| **5.** | 3 | **19.** | 17 | **33.** | 5 | **47.** | 6 |
| **6.** | 12 | **20.** | 15 | **34.** | 12 | **48.** | 18 |
| **7.** | 2 | **21.** | 11 | **35.** | 13 | **49.** | 10 |
| **8.** | 5 | **22.** | 4 | **36.** | 9 | **50.** | 16 |
| **9.** | 7 | **23.** | 9 | **37.** | 4 | **51.** | 7 |
| **10.** | 10 | **24.** | 9 | **38.** | 11 | **52.** | 9 |
| **11.** | 9 | **25.** | 14 | **39.** | 8 | **53.** | 5 |
| **12.** | 6 | **26.** | 15 | **40.** | 7 | **54.** | 3 |
| **13.** | 4 | **27.** | 12 | **41.** | 0 | **55.** | 12 |
| **14.** | 3 | **28.** | 8 | **42.** | 8 | **56.** | 11 |

## Missing Addend

**1.** 8
**2.** 3
**3.** 6
**4.** 5
**5.** 10
**6.** 3
**7.** 1
**8.** 1
**9.** 1
**10.** 3
**11.** 5
**12.** 7
**13.** 3
**14.** 7
**15.** 4
**16.** 0
**17.** 10
**18.** 5
**19.** 6
**20.** 0
**21.** 0
**22.** 4
**23.** 7
**24.** 5
**25.** 9
**26.** 1
**27.** 0
**28.** 0
**29.** 1
**30.** 3
**31.** 2
**32.** 1
**33.** 5
**34.** 1
**35.** 2
**36.** 3
**37.** 1
**38.** 9
**39.** 0
**40.** 0
**41.** 7
**42.** 9
**43.** 8
**44.** 8
**45.** 8
**46.** 5
**47.** 10
**48.** 3
**49.** 7
**50.** 1
**51.** 10
**52.** 0
**53.** 8
**54.** 9
**55.** 2
**56.** 7
**57.** 5
**58.** 7
**59.** 9
**60.** 1
**61.** 10
**62.** 1
**63.** 0
**64.** 6
**65.** 1
**66.** 3
**67.** 2
**68.** 0

## Add 3 numbers within 20

**1.** 11
**2.** 10
**3.** 11
**4.** 8
**5.** 18
**6.** 16
**7.** 14
**8.** 12
**9.** 18
**10.** 11
**11.** 15
**12.** 8
**13.** 11
**14.** 7
**15.** 11
**16.** 11
**17.** 6
**18.** 19
**19.** 7
**20.** 3

## Subtracting within 0-10

**1.** 3
**2.** 0
**3.** 3
**4.** 0
**5.** 1
**6.** 6
**7.** 1
**8.** 0
**9.** 0
**10.** 7
**11.** 1
**12.** 0
**13.** 2
**14.** 0
**15.** 4
**16.** 1
**17.** 0
**18.** 9
**19.** 2
**20.** 2
**21.** 8

**22.** 3
**23.** 1
**24.** 0
**25.** 10
**26.** 6
**27.** 3
**28.** 3
**29.** 4
**30.** 3
**31.** 1
**32.** 1
**33.** 5
**34.** 1
**35.** 4
**36.** 0
**37.** 2
**38.** 2
**39.** 3
**40.** 2
**41.** 3
**42.** 3
**43.** 0
**44.** 6
**45.** 4
**46.** 2
**47.** 3
**48.** 0
**49.** 10
**50.** 0
**51.** 6
**52.** 4
**53.** 0
**54.** 0
**55.** 2
**56.** 7
**57.** 1
**58.** 0
**59.** 6
**60.** 2
**61.** 4
**62.** 0
**63.** 4
**64.** 1
**65.** 8
**66.** 0
**67.** 1
**68.** 1

## Missing Minuend or Subtrahend

**1.** 0
**2.** 3
**3.** 9
**4.** 0
**5.** 1
**6.** 1
**7.** 8
**8.** 8
**9.** 2
**10.** 3
**11.** 0
**12.** 2
**13.** 8
**14.** 0
**15.** 5
**16.** 4
**17.** 1
**18.** 3
**19.** 6
**20.** 1
**21.** 6
**22.** 0
**23.** 1
**24.** 1
**25.** 5
**26.** 7
**27.** 9
**28.** 7
**29.** 0
**30.** 4
**31.** 4
**32.** 2
**33.** 9
**34.** 1
**35.** 1
**36.** 7
**37.** 3
**38.** 4
**39.** 9
**40.** 1
**41.** 3
**42.** 1
**43.** 7
**44.** 0
**45.** 3
**46.** 0
**47.** 3
**48.** 6
**49.** 9
**50.** 2
**51.** 4
**52.** 0
**53.** 5
**54.** 1
**55.** 0
**56.** 3

www.ingramcontent.com/pod-product-compliance
Lightning Source LLC
LaVergne TN
LVHW060627170826
845677LV00027B/1756